D1600688

Dear Mark

poems

Martin Rock

Brooklyn Arts Press · New York

Dear Mark
© 2013 Martin Rock

ISBN-13: 978-1-936767-19-9

Cover art & interior word art by Aaron Sing Fox; interior assemblages by Martin Rock. Cover design by Martin Rock & Joe Pan.

Published in The United States of America by:
Brooklyn Arts Press
154 N 9th St #1
Brooklyn, NY 11249
www.BrooklynArtsPress.com
info@brooklynartspress.com

Distributed to the trade by Small Press Distribution / SPD
www.spdbooks.org

Library of Congress Cataloging-in-Publication Data

Rock, Martin.
 [Poems. Selections]
 Dear Mark : poems / by Martin Rock.
     pages cm
 "Distributed to the trade by Small Press Distribution / SPD"--T. p. verso.
 ISBN 978-1-936767-19-9 (Paperback : alk. paper)
 1. Rothko, Mark, 1903-1970--Poetry. I. Title.

 PS3618.O35435D43 2013
 811'.6--dc23

                         201300419

FIRST EDITION

The author would like to acknowledge Mark Rothko and his paintings, without which none of these poems would exist. Many thanks as well to Joe Pan at Brooklyn Arts Press for putting this book into the world, to Brian Trimboli for getting me started writing this project, and to the editors of the following journals, in which these poems were initially published:

At-Large Magazine: "White Center, 1950"; "Red, Orange,
        Tan, & Purple, 1949"
The Bakery: "No. 61, Rust & Blue, 1953"; "Ochre & Red on
        Red, 1954"; "No. 9, Dark Over Light Earth, 1954";
        "No. 9, White & Black on Wine, 1958"; "No. 43,
        Mauve, 1960"; "No. 1, Black Form, 1964"; "No. 7,
        Black Form, 1964"
InDigest: "No. 14, White & Greens in Blue, 1957"
Jellyroll: "Earth & Green, 1955"; "Untitled, 1957"
Leveler: "No. 8, Black Form, 1964"

"Untitled, 1957" first appeared in *Apocalypse Anthology* (Flying Guillotine Press).

CONTENTS

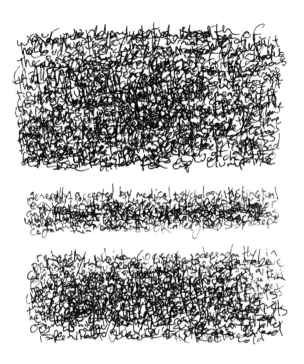

In all chaos there is a cosmos, in all disorder a secret order.

-C.G. Jung-

Certain people always say we should go back to nature.
I notice they never say we should go forward to nature.

-Mark Rothko-

No. 5 / No. 22, 1949

In the mustard sky
        clouds have gathered
    inside a box

of Plexiglas.
        The horizon
    smolders cadmium

from some blast,
        & we're standing
    so far away

the buildings appear
        scarcely a layer
    of fur:

hackles stood up
        in a bog of light.
    All that remains

of the city
        are three jellyfish
    tendrils,

flagella floating
        on the surface
    of the ocean.

What's missing
        is an animal
    to bless

with the paradox
          of motion: halving,
     & then, arrival.

Four hovering
          spots of light
     in the sky

& there is nearly
          enough time
     to paint a door

which may
          or may not
     open

onto
          a suitable
     afternoon.

We are only
          beginning
     our time here

& already
          the curtain
     is boiling.

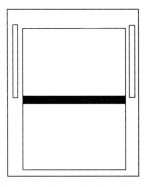

Red, Orange, Tan, & Purple, 1949

You've given your robot payot
& the mantle is bleeding from its ears.

This fire is the cleavage of two planets:
gods set to destroy each other, that they may join.

For now, a splinter of peace between them,
which is also a device to measure the decibels

when they crash. Nothing is funny about a mustache
that won't grow in, or a thin black line

when it shivers. Ours is the flaxen planet.
Our window is a hole in the tooth of your golem,

who reinvents himself an opening in the wall,
ushers us through, & ghosts himself away.

Something heavy grows inside the earth.
I'd like to unearth it. I'd like to unearth them all.

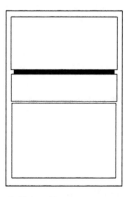

White Center, 1950

In your landscapes we drown
or are stuck between layers of earth.
Here is a film of crude oil on the ocean,
& the beach is cake icing or snow
near to melting. We are content
to be taken in by your rectangular sun,
the misshapen god of our fathers.
The butterfly's body is also a urinal cake
with antennae & legs braided into a rope.
Black line what separates our species
from the encroaching sky, & why again
is there a spot of red on its brow?
There are a thousand places I'd rather be
& I have left them all to be here.

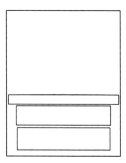

Blue, Green, & Brown, 1952

The future has four horizons:
            the Gate,
    the Echo, the Landlord,

& the Mansion.
            Open the incinerator
    that is your mouth

& we shall enter as bread.
            The stuff of existence
    is shoveled down

by hungry ghosts, throats so tight
            even the sand
    cannot squeeze through.

Beneath the rawboned brow,
            eyes spatter oil:
    an ancient blue joke

smeared onto indigo cheeks.
            Under the silver clay,
    under the glaucous earth,

under the Prussian-blue sky
            rests a box
        filled with letters

known themselves to death.
                Where the first sky
        meets the first ocean

floats a legion of welders.
                Slip now your silent frame
        into the foam.

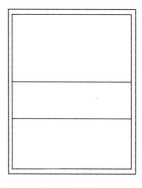

No. 61, Rust & Blue, 1953

Down the path, a barn has left its lights on.

    We're lying on the red clay & it is cold

against my cheeks & eyes the barn

    atomic in the distance. Families are huddled

in partitions underground I fear

    we're one of them. In front of us, four wisps

are dancing transparent blue children

    against corroded brick. A storm is rolling in.

You've left handprints in the sky,

    which is also a bakers' pin intended to flatten

the earth. Your device is all hair & no eyes.

    As a child you waited for a beard

& now we're lost inside its knot.

    The blood on your golem's mask has dried.

Ochre & Red on Red, 1954

A screen door beyond
    which the beloved

scholar has been put to death.
    Our ancestors' paint

was their medicine,
    yellow paste of rabbit skin

glue & chalk—bits
    of the earth, yellow ochre,

toxic orpiment—ingested
    to enter the sun.

The eyes of our military
    are pressed together;

one seeps from the other,
    a malformed zygote

hell-bent on devouring its twin.
    Here is the earth,

flattened & laid out to dry
   over the flattened sun.

What we perceive is time
    passed through a mandoline,

a segment of the worm
   that eats through the body.

The ancients painted themselves,
   their walls: one vanished

into the other. We watch
   them move through the screen,

each one of the faces
   tormented to be the sky.

You have disappeared
   a feral cat into the paint.

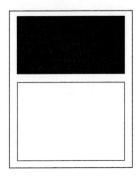

No. 9, Dark Over Light Earth, 1954

The night is earth piled on earth
                 & all buried things are peering in.
   A face presses against the glass

of your basement window,
                 a body on its hands & knees
   breathes fog & writes in glossolalia.

It seems you view daytime as heavier
                 than night. If not heavier, more solid.
   Night is diaphanous, is nothing more

than ten-billion years of light lost
                 to the opposite side of the earth,
   which ends. The earth ends.

Children learn features first, find emotion
                 in the eyes, the brow, the skin;
   our brain remembers faces into your paint.

According to the Mishradic position,
                 we spend our lives reacquainting ourselves
   with lost knowledge.

In utero we are taught by angels,
                 who strike us on the soft beneath the nose,
   that we forget.

Earth & Green, 1955

Here is a mass grave tunneled
through the collective childhood:

In the red pit a transparent woman
searches serenely for the other half

of her face, her torso a misshapen turkey,
plucked for eating.

In the gallery, three feathers
that must have passed from the painting

float to the ground, fragments
of a parallel world: disjointed moons

spun out of orbit. Suspended here,
incorporeal bodies outside of time.

There is a buffer of blue smoke
between the two worlds: a snake

with the head of a child, coiled
like a watch spring on the grass.

Green the wallpaper that killed Napoleon;
green the secret fire, the living spirit of matter.

Red is the last color seen by the eye,
the longest wavelength, the insect

cochineal ground into food
& lipstick, an ancient living paint.

All the original shadows are here,
& the distinct profile

of a man's body, slumped
in front of a dark window in prayer.

No. 20, Deep Red & Black, 1957

Instead of a soccer field, a patch of grass
the size & shape of a soccer field

has been razed. Present the thing
& take it away: what language does.

Where the bleachers aren't,
a hole dug into the earth has no bed.

To play, one must step into the air
above the pit. In an attempt to bring rain,

hooligans have stamped ash
into the shape of a black calf. The robot

is rusted through, or cherry red & hot
to trot. Your golem shows his face again,

& wears a great Russian hat, & everywhere
a mouth should be it isn't. Above him,

the sky is on fire, as though someone forgot
to plug the hole left by the evening sun.

Here is a map of simultaneity: we begin
by breathing, & work ourselves to death.

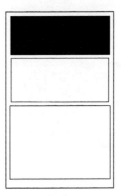

Untitled, 1957

Life is a kind of rust.
Here is a vertical future
& buildings rise
like sandstone karsts
or a cross obscured
by the darkness around it.
There are no windows
& the doors are thin
as burlap. Behind them,
people do terrible things
to one another
as the young lounge
wildly on the grass.
In a cubicle, a man
is dragged across the floor,
his head the eye of a giant fish.
This time, your golem
is a Cyclops, unhappy
to be so thin.
Blood contains too much
iron & reacts violently
with oxygen. Such is life.
A beautiful woman,

eyes cast toward the earth,
is mourning the loss
of one of her favorite mittens.
The mushroom cloud
is also a clown face
& a skeleton dances
to an invisible marionette.

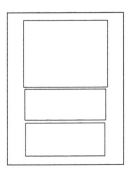

No. 14, White & Greens in Blue, 1957

There are dragonflies in the primordial soup again.
        Low-lying clouds the white beard of the golem,
known affectionately as the Potentate of Pigment.
    It tells a story from top to bottom:

black to greenish black, to white: a weight inverted,
        one narrative of color that casts the sky in shadow.
One of the fallen gods holds his lover at night
    under one arm, surf crashing primitively at his feet.

He steps into the ocean, subtracts himself to a single cell,
        & begins to split. Today in history:
ABIOGENETIC BULLS STAMPEDE WHITEWATER.
    Then, cooling & jellyfish, or was it a mushroom cloud

the size of Kansas the size of a mushroom?
        Everything is set in soft blue. Thank you for this.
Blue is the pearl that slips through the fog,
    the blue light of awareness, the blue head of birth.

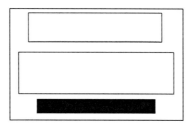

No. 9, White & Black on Wine, 1958

The door is mantled
            in rust & prisoners
      receive their meals

through a dark slot.
            We stand behind
      an opaque cardinal

glass, suffering
            in all this
      wine.

To mollify our keeper,
            we've developed
      a new language

based on the subtleties
            of color.
      Rather than speak,

we stand naked
            before one another
      & blush

while dismantling
                  a pomegranate.
      Here

communication began,
                in blood
      seen through the skin,

in bloom.
                The inmates
      are terrorized

into cheerfulness.
                In the cell,
      mergansers

flying east,
                & a woman
      lies in the sun

with blindingly exposed
                breasts.
      One of the men

inlays pearl:
                luxuriant couple
      making love

in the bath.
                The woman licks
      his neck

& on the body of a spider
                death's head
      is near.

A god has poked holes
            in the sheets
    above the sky

& the golem is there,
            eyeing
    the world again.

Black on Maroon, 1958

Here is the map by which is planned
a retreat from the world of form
into the eternal plane of reflected light.
Between the lines, a body stands
with his back to us, shoulders slumped
& head turned that we see an eye in shadow,
a face fallen into collapse. Horizontal
smears are broken sutras: flesh attempting
to hold itself together. Heavy iron bars
come down hard on a swollen foot,
& behind the bars, shadowy figures hide
like cartoon prisoners made real
by their reconciliation to flatness.
In the darkness beyond the sun, chaos
continues to organize itself into faces,
& faces continue to organize themselves
into sentience. If you're reading this,
may you find all of my faults and tell
no one. The old man's beard is long
enough in which to drown. The child
with a pelican chin watches us stoically,
as though it is we who do not exist.

Black on Maroon, 1959

Uncanny expression of
  two bodies
pull at the other's skin
  Architect and builder,
on a corrugated
    Father of two
intent on dismantling
  abstract memory
lying next to each other
    There is nowhere
is already full of bodies
  Time is a product
  fills his space
  & without warning,
In the exploding present
which stops billions

electromagnetism:
viewed from above
  by way of skin.
  thick iron bars left
    tin roof.
brooding children
  each other's inheritance:
of twins
  in a house without floors.
to fall & the earth
  emptied.
of change: a man
with belongings,
  passes them on.
    here is the symbol
  of devices by touch.

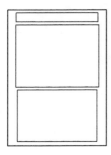

No. 43, Mauve, 1960

Forbearance is no longer a word
        than is ascoliasm, in which medieval
children beat each other to tatters.

The contortionist has fit everything
        but her head into the box
& her body's turned to vapor.

Like a cloud woven into the future,
        the point of your exclamation
mark is in the process of exploding.

Finally, we have the wherewithal
        to fit the maroon sky
into an aquarium that floats

a balloon above our blanket
        in the ash. "Dirty snow"
is such a relative phrase, the earth

is colder than a meat locker
        in the middle of summer,
which is to be the new aggregate

of all previous seasons.
        We have learned to tell time
by reading the shadows cast

by the sun what's disappeared
        into the dust & spice. Everything
smells of cinnamon, & hyssop.

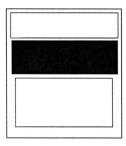

No. 10, Brown, Black, Sienna on Dark Wine, 1963

Here is a trap door into the skull.

Phrenology is a philosophy
of division from the fascist past

& our attention is focused
on The Carnivorous Instinct
& The Organ of Religion.

In the dark panel, a man
shaped like a mushroom
divides himself into territories.
Above him, the epoch of desert

has risen.
He welds shut the passages
& revamps into the light.
I envision myself a pilgrim
at your chapel

& stand in front of you
as you have stood
in front of me. Your black
is thinner than rust,

& I can feel it studying us
at the window which has no pane.
Everything is trapped inside itself

& there is a benevolent face
in the clouds roiling above

this calm wind in the ash.

No. 1, Black Form, 1964

If we are to believe Kandinsky, black
is like the silence of the body after death.
The hole you've cut in our metal roof
leads to a future in which we have reached
a false objective: there are no objects,
& corporeality does not exist even in language.
Having nothing to speak them, words
dematerialize, though even *this* is inaccurate.
In the field, there is no field. In mind, no mind.
As for the silence after death, we hear it
behind the wall behind your painting.
What Kandinsky named silence, you paint.
In front of the obsidian monolith a man
in a canoe rows himself considerably away.

No. 7, Black Form, 1964

Raven desired a doorway to language
so he turned himself into a grain of sand
& crawled inside your glass of water.

He grew inside you until every color was influenced
by his thirst to speak. In this mythology,
pillars of smoke outside your window:

a dark planet perceived as the coming of night.
The clouded roman helmet is also a feather
& the faces have crows' feet mewling

from their eyes. Stare at an unchanging object
and you cause change around it. So prove the stars.
Remain fixed & the future approaches as liquid

& all is swallowed. So shows the river. Here we kneel
to drink. Here our skulls fuse like bottles in the fire.

No. 8, Black Form, 1964

Like Malevich's black
               square,
     the future is full

of devices that sleep
               & devices
     that inhabit sleep.

Hordes of blackflies
               flown
     from your cellar

into the shadows
               we track
     to know the world

exists.
               A thick layer
     of soot rests

over our eye-
               lids & we stand
     inside a giant

briquette
               & stretch
     into the hole

in your terrarium.
               We make ends
     meet.

The tornado
            that swept through
      Brooklyn

began inside
            your house:
      inside the box

that you have
            not allowed
      light

inside your house.
            Your golem
      is here

& smokes
            cigarettes
      in a lighthouse

& emits
            dark matter
      by which

we are to find him.
            We are time-
      travelers.

In sleep
            our bodies are full
      of wormholes.

Untitled, 1968

The Haz–Mat team has arrived & this is the last

    I will write you often.

I'm looking out the window of a marigold jet;

        the sky is duke blue,

cloudless as Ryokan's enlightened brains: he dreamt

    of white ash in fall, outside

the past & future. Your vision of eternity is similar:

        an aquarium buried

in autumn wheat. The fish are invisible in the present

    moment, though we can attend

to the wake left by their fins. What is unending

        has followed you to us

& for a moment we are blameless. Death settles

a body between frames

& you appear sometimes in one, sometimes in another.

Why must everyone leave the pool

from the same side? What is the use

of a vessel in which no substance gathers?

When an object enters a black hole,

it stretches like the faces in your cornfield.

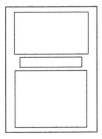

Serigraph, Acrylic on Paper, 1968

There are two of us in the room.

        Or there is one
& we are cut in half
    by the bending of light

        in gallons of paint.
Of the great beak's
    two planes,

the upper has been pried open

        to reveal
an expanse of beach
    before land was spoken.

        As mud,
your golem hated it here, before
    the disjointing

which was this painting's birth.

        Guns hidden
in the forest
    & there is a duck

     under a microscope
 & an armored mask
   under the duck.

There is a crumb of myself

    in the dandelion
in which I am hiding.
   Something is opening

    its face
at eye level & I am
   peering from it.

There is a spot of blood on your right eyelid.

NOTES:

p. 15 – "The Gate, the Echo, the Landlord, & the Mansion" is taken from the poem "The Golem" by Jorge Luis Borges. In addition to "the Key," this is Borges' description of the secret Name which, when uttered, is capable of creating life.

p. 15 – Hungry ghosts (from the Chinese 餓鬼, or *èguǐ*) are Mahayana Buddhist beings who experience a supernatural degree of suffering due to exceptionally narrow throats and extreme hunger. They are also known as *preta*.

p. 20, 30 – These poems reference Carl Sagan's hypothesis that the human mind is "hard-wired" from birth to identify the human face, which is one explanation for the frequency with which people see faces in instances of pareidolia.

p. 21 – Napoleon's green wallpaper is thought to have poisoned him due to the use of Scheele's Green, a pigment which, when exposed to heat and dampness, exudes the poisonous vapor arsenic trimethyl.

pg. 26 – The Hindu Vedas refer to the Blue Pearl, or the divine light of Consciousness, a blue light the size of a sesame seed that appears between the eyes during meditation.

p. 33 – "The Carnivorous Instinct; the Tendency to Murder" & "The Organ of Religion" are 2 of the 27 "organs" of the brain identified by Franz Joseph Gall in his work on phrenology, *The Anatomy and Physiology of the Nervous System in General, and of the Brain in Particular, with Observations upon the possibility of ascertaining the several Intellectual and Moral Dispositions of Man and Animal, by the configuration of their Heads.*

p. 34 – The phrase "[black] is like the silence of the body after death" is taken directly from Wassily Kandinsky's book, *On the Spiritual in Art.*

p. 35 – This poem relies heavily on a Pacific Northwest First Nations creation myth in which Raven, who lives in a world of darkness, turns himself into a grain of sand to be swallowed by a young woman who dwells in the house of light.

MARTIN ROCK is a poet, editor, and teacher living in Brooklyn. He lived in Japan for nearly four years, where he taught elementary and junior high school and studied Japanese. His poetry has appeared or is forthcoming in *Black Warrior Review; Conduit; DIAGRAM; Forklift, Ohio; H_NGM_N; Third Coast; The Journal*, and was included in *Best New Poets 2012* and featured recently on the websites *Brooklyn Poets* and *The Bakery.* With Philip D. Ischy, he wrote the chapbook *Fish, You Bird* (Pilot 2010). He has served as Editor in Chief of *Washington Square*, as Managing Editor of *Epiphany*, and is currently Editor in Chief of *Loaded Bicycle.* The recipient of fellowships from New York University, Port Townsend Writers Conference, and University of Houston, he will soon move to Texas to begin a doctoral candidacy in literature and creative writing.